About the Author

I am an Oriental medicine healer at Positive Life Acupuncture in Warwick, NY, a converted Catholic and a writer living in the remote wilderness of north New Jersey. These stories were inspired and written originally for my brother, who suffered from bipolar and addiction disorder, and have been added to after my experience with beautiful souls willing to share their feelings with me.

Collection of Emotionful Stories

Nicole Allegretti

Collection of Emotionful Stories

Olympia Publishers
London

www.olympiapublishers.com
OLYMPIA PAPERBACK EDITION

Copyright © Nicole Allegretti 2023

The right of Nicole Allegretti to be identified as author of
this work has been asserted in accordance with sections 77 and 78 of
the Copyright, Designs and Patents Act 1988.

A CIP catalogue record for this title is
available from the British Library.

ISBN: 978-1-80439-521-9

This is a work of fiction.
Names, characters, places and incidents originate from the writer's
imagination. Any resemblance to actual persons, living or dead, is
purely coincidental.

First Published in 2023

Olympia Publishers
Tallis House
2 Tallis Street
London
EC4Y 0AB

Printed in Great Britain

Dedication

For my brother, Dougie, and for you, my friend.

Acknowledgements

My gratitude to Stef, Aura, my mom in heaven and my dad, who always support me and my writing. My love to Dan for being there, in the unseen.

I Am the Tree, and These Pages are Me

An old man took a walk-through trees in the park.

"I stomp the trees
Even when they say please,
Trample their dreams,
With just my tiny squeeze, a button that wakes them
From their sleep with a bang.
You see, the goal is power,
No other point.
Power to be,
Power to see,
Power to fly,
Power to multiply.
In this big world today,
For to do anything,
We each need power and I'll make sure I've got it."

Suddenly he listened.
A small voice made a sound.

"But what about the trees? Where will we play?"

The old man laughed.
"No time for play,
Young boy, no time at all.

In this land work and work, toil and dig up the soil.
It's money that's the goal,
Money, power,
Power to be,
Power to see,
Power to fly,
Power to multiply.
Don't you want to be, young boy? Have the power to see?
Have the power to fly? And one day, multiply?"

The young boy sat and thought. He scratched his head.
"I do," said the boy, "but…"
"But what?" said the old man.
"Will we have time to play?" the boy asked him.
"You won't want time to play. You will have everything
That you have ever dreamed of."
He leaned in, his eyes grew wide,
And he whispered,
"All the power in the world."

The boy followed the man,
And learned a lot from him,
And one day found himself
In an office
Where the trees used to be
As high up as the clouds.
He looked down from his tall square glass window,
He thought he did have all the power in the world.
He walked outside,
To where the few trees lived. He spotted a young boy
Sitting under a tree

Playing games with the leaves.

He asked the boy,
Like he was asked before, "In this land, work and work, toil
and dig up the soil.
It's money that's the goal,
Money, power,
Power to be,
Power to see,
Power to fly,
Power to multiply.
Don't you want to be, young boy? Have the power to see?
Have the power to fly? And one day, multiply?"
He leaned in, his eyes grew wide,
And he whispered,
"All the power in the world."

"No, dad," the young boy said, "I want to play in trees."

The man became confused
And was startled
By his response.
The little boy
found himself as a man
In a gray suit
And a gray tie
Dressed with a sigh
With the power to see
Over the tallest trees
In his grand office space,
With the power to be

In this vast place,
With the power to fly
Over the fastest race,
And power to multiply
His newfound faith.
And he remembered when
He was a boy
Playing under the trees.
His eyes saddened
And he soon realized
That he had lost something,
Something that couldn't be found.
He sat under the tree
Watching his son's smile.
He began to remember.

"I had lost something that
Couldn't be found,
But I somehow
Have found it right
Here in the ground."

He laughed and played
And then became aware
That he had always had ability to care,
And he had always had
Power to be,
Power to see,
Power to fly,
And multiply,

Every day, all along.

"What have you found?" asked the boy.
"Something that cannot be lost,
Something that cannot be gained,
It cannot be fought for,
Nor found in fame.
It is my spirit, you see. I am the tree,
The tree is me."

Christmas Light

"He's gray and grumpy,
He's old and frumpy,
And sad and weary,
Mopey and dreary,
Are you sure we want to visit him on Christmas Day?
I'd rather you take me in the sleigh."

"To protect his heart, it must be
Hidden from all to see,
Except perhaps, from you and me.

It appears as though
He doesn't see or know
His own warmth and light,
Deep within, shines bright. It's bonded, it's sewn,
Kept away, not fully grown.

It may be hidden and square,
Gray or not found anywhere, deep down,
I promise it's there,
It may be stuffed down so far,
Deep in some old, knotted scar

Light and warmth is what we'll send,
It may be risky to lend

Out a hand to him right now.
It may be out of reach,
It may need to be unlearned to teach,
It may be buried in his speech,
Through the crackles and hardness,
The anger and bossiness,
But we'll soon find a softness,
He can make right this wrongness.

We'll go and visit, bring some hot tea, share in the spirit,
A family we'll be.
We'll sit and listen,
Next to a fire of color,
Share light with one another,
The way to change anger and sorrow, bring the person into
tomorrow,
Let him see the light within you and me, the reflection will
allow him to see.
A hearty smile, and a warm connection better than any other
perfection.

He's your grandfather, you see,
I couldn't tell you before,
I wasn't willing and neither was he. He was very angry for a
time, became sad on top of that,
But he was great for a rhyme, he could write and play,
He could sing and dance,
That was back in the old days,
When he was new in his ways.
Since then, grandmom had passed, he didn't want to talk to
the rest. This Christmas will be different,

I can feel it today,
Are you ready to go for a visit,
Even if getting turned down, we may?"

"We walked down the path
All snowy and covered,
One that seemed familiar to me,
Old memories discovered.
When he opened the door, I saw an old man,
I was told he was my grandfather,
The door he did slam.
I looked up at my mother
And I could see in her eyes,
Sadness and all the unsuccessful tries,
I knocked again, this time very loudly,
My mother just stood, in silence proudly.
"Grandpa, it's me!" I yelled and I yelled,
When he opened the door, I could see
Why he had slammed it in front of me.
His eyes were all red and tearing,
Just like my mother's next to me,
They gave each other one look,
And with a hug,
They cried so much they shook.
Then my grandfather looked down at me,
I thought I must be in some trouble,
He knelt down and hugged me with glee.

What happened next was confusing at most,
He wiped his eyes and held the door open,
Made us hot cocoa, and sat for a toast.

Mother was right, there was a fire,
And grandfather told stories,
He seemed never to tire. He played his old fiddle,
We danced to the sounds,
And every which way,
Smiles were all around.

I couldn't believe
He had been alone for so long,
When all we had to do was see
The light that's inside you and in me,
The reflection is what let him see.

From that night on,
He was no longer alone
So brightly his light shone.
For he had the knack, he could always tell when someone
was sad and alone,
He would sit beside them, and listen well.

He opened his doors to visitors and friends
To family and loved ones, making amends.
From that day on,
The holidays were filled with love and delight,
All because of that Christmas of hope, and a miracle of
light."

A Song's Rhymeness

"Kindness is gone from the smiles,
Laughter does not go on for miles,
Songs, they don't seem to rhyme,
The sun no longer shines.

And I'm changing things
You may be thinking, how?
I'm getting rid of the smiles
And throwing away the songs
And blocking that dim sun.
What's the point to it all?"

"But, my friend,
I see the kindness in smiles
And hear the laughter for miles,
I hear the songs that rhyme,
And feel the sun that shines.

It may just be you that does not see,
Maybe if I show you a different way,
We can change it, yes, that's the key."

"Show me a different way?
Why, what on earth do you mean?
I see the way I see,

And that, my friend, will not sway.
The earth is solid,
The sky is too,
See this piece of wood,
It makes a sound when I knock,
Just like it should.

But without smiles that are kind
And songs that rhyme
And a sun that shines,
And laughter heard for miles,
I cannot leave things as they are.

The world around me, it must change.
I must say though, it is very strange
That you can see all these things
And I cannot."

"Let's go on a journey,
And after it I promise
If you do not once again see I will help you
Get rid of the smiles that are not kind,
And block out the sun that no longer shines,
We will throw away the songs that don't rhyme,
And cancel the laughter not heard for miles.

What do you say?"

"Well, all right, I suppose,
Although I don't see how
Such a journey will come to a close."

"Don't worry about that, just follow me,
We will walk this way and that way,
And turn this corner, you'll see,
Here it is, now you must be silent, what you are about to see,
Comes with a great deal of quiet.

It comes with years of time
Of waiting and growing
And years of working,
Loving and sowing.

It will awaken both you and me
To the wonders of this world,
To the smiles of kindness,
To the songs rhymeness,
To the sun that shines,
And the laughter heard for miles."

"What is it there? It just seems like a nest
A little bird's eggs all covered to her best.

I still don't see how this is supposed to help,
My friend, I think our journey is for naught."

Suddenly his eyes grew larger than large,
They began to water just a little,
The smallest tear turned into a trickle.
The eggs that just seemed like eggs in a nest
Began to crack and open and whistle.

He saw their tiny faces begin to emerge
What was this! It seemed like a surge
Of love and hope, all things did merge.

Suddenly he watched as the mama came down
She cuddled her babies with the tiniest sound.

After this day, they did return,
And watched quietly and silently,
Soon, this journey was done,
And it was time to discern.
"My friend, I am not convinced, that was truly beautiful to
see, and I thank you for taking me,
But I have not seen what I long to see."

His eyes filled with anger
And his throat wallowed up with fear
That he may never again hear,
Or see, or feel such things.

As he stormed off and away,
One of the birds began to sing she perched on his shoulder,
And sang the most beautiful rhyme he'd heard from this
world over,
It was filled with highs and lows and felt just so with his
woes,
So much so that he no longer felt alone.

And with that song, through the trees
The sun began to shine so brightly,
He forgot all his troubles,

And smiled mightily,
And with that his friend smiled back,
He saw the kindness that he once did lack,

He and his friend laughed and laughed for miles
at the thought of not seeing the kindness in smiles, and the
thought of not feeling the sun shining,
Or hearing the songs rhyming.

He felt surprised
When he soon realized
That the problem he faced
Was meant to bring him
To this wondrous place.

Where he could once again
See the kindness in smiles, feel the sun that shines, hear the
song's rhymes,
And hear the laughter for miles.

This journey didn't lead him to see all that he had lost
But showed him what always was, to listen was the only cost.

The Monster in My Closet

There are scary branches
And waving monsters
That come out at night
I wish I could squander,
They moan and groan
With the best of their scariness
It has me hiding under my bed
The most scary I've felt
The most dread
It's going to get me,
It's going to eat me,
Maybe it's just here to scare
And watch while I hide
I don't even know what it is
It's a monster for sure maybe it's a giant squid
That lives out of water
It came up inland
And now doesn't know how to get back
So it just scares little girls and boys,
In hopes of finding some joy.
Maybe it's a big bear
That doesn't know how to get home
So he just roams and roams
And screams and moans
Or maybe it's a giant snake

That's going to eat me in one bite
It just has to open its mouth
It just might happen, it might.
Maybe it's a spider
He may begin small
But then he grows tall,
That crawls around
Just to find my feet
Without making a sound.

Whatever it is
It's in my closet I'm sure
I looked in to find its eyes
And felt the fear of all fears
Well up inside.

Wait a minute,
I sat and thought for a moment
And remembered
I am strong too
I can face this fear, I can, yes I can too.

I thought I needed to get away,
But maybe I didn't,
Maybe what I really needed,
Was to stay.

I looked that monster square in the eye
And I yelled "I'm not afraid of you!"
And to my disbelief, he gave a sigh
He shrugged and said "What's the use! I would rather have a

truce
Than scare and scream
And make a scene
I'm tired you see,
I've been doing this too long
 It's really not me,
I love laughter and smiles
And children who talk for miles."
The old monster sat down
With a big, long frown,
And I saw something
I never thought I would,
I saw that old monster cry,
Like an old monster should.
He put out his hand and I mine,
We shook each other's for the first time
It was a moment,
I'm sure one of its kind.
I couldn't decide after that
If I should be scared
So I threw down a blanket,
For the old monster to sleep on,
And threw down some more
In case the others weren't gone. That night I watched him sleep
He didn't make a peep,
He seemed exhausted
And I guess he was,
All that scaring and blaring
A heart that just needed some love.

From that night on, mother would always ask
Why put so many blankets out? I started to explain the task
Over breakfast one day,
I told her about the monsters
And how they just needed some rest,
So they wouldn't be so scared when put to the test,
They were overworked you see
No time for themselves to just be,
I guess that happens to all of us,
Not just to me.

She just nodded and um hummed,
And went back to making breakfast. I knew at that moment,
That I would never again fear
And so let me be clear,
What I thought was a monster,
Did turn out to be real
I just realized that being afraid
Wasn't the only way to feel.
Next time you're afraid
Of a monster, a bear or a squid,
Maybe it comes from the closet
No matter where your monster has hid
You can choose to face your fear
Just as I did.

Specifically You

Two birds sat on a branch,
One looked very well kept
Her feathers full of fluff and
Her nest very well swept,
The other, a little disheveled,
And maybe a little more affected
By little things like the weather. One bird said the other,
"Most people wouldn't guess
But I feel in myself less
Less than the stars less than the birds
Less than that person there,
And less than that perfectly edged square.
I don't know where it came from
But I feel it's there. It's a part of me
That I want to cast away
To Let go of and never
Again towards it sway."

"My friend,
I've heard this before
I don't know if it's true for you
But I'll repeat it once more.
All of You is you
No matter if it's bad or good, or when you're feeling blue.
I'll say this, I don't know if I should,

Maybe if you give me a nod I could.
If we begin to love that part
Of us that we so long to cast away I think that's the start,
To feel peace, when towards we sway.
It's a piece of you, just a part,
And you my friend are truly true
And You are wonderful
And sometimes, even blue
But this is lovely and beautiful too. All of this is part of being
And in a way truly seeing. We've all felt this way
And that way,
You feel these things
It doesn't make you less than,
It makes you quite good,
As sharing feelings would. We're all in this together.
No one is less than,
No one is better than,
More of a mess than,
Or more blessed than.
And I'm sorry you've felt that before,
But it's not at all what you have in store,
For this life will bring you twists and turns,
It will bring feelings of loss and love,
And may even give you a shove,
But surely,
There's no less than
No better than,
No more of a mess than,
No one more blessed than. And if you say I am
Then I have for you a question, who can say who is better
than? Or less than?

Or more of a mess than? Or more blessed than?
Who can compare
Him and him and her and her,
Him and her, and her and him,
This and that, and that and this,
There and here, and here and there? Whoever says they can,
Has decided too much
For that is the way
To begin down a spiraling tunnel of such, a tunnel to lead
To an unending feed
Of approval,
And eventually
The removal
Of all that makes you you,
The beauty, the blues,
The sadness, even when you lose,
Those specific ways
That make you specifically you,
Beautifully you,
The unique things that you do,
That make you uniquely you,
Fantastically you.
The happy, the glad,
The laughter, even the mad. Next time you're feeling blue
And less than, and untrue
Just remember that
There is nothing and no one that can make you feel
Less than,
Better than,
More of a mess than,
Or more blessed than,

Except, perhaps, you."

The one bird
Looked up with a smile
When she finally realized that
She wasn't less than
She wasn't better than
More of a mess than
Or more blessed than,
She was enough
Just as she was. If you remember,
In the beginning,
We never said which bird was who,
Did the story give you a clue?
Take a moment,
Outside of the way you see,
Yes that's the key,
Outside of the way you see.

The Bird and the Stone

One morning a young girl
Was on her way to school
Driving with her father
Like every morning past
They turned a corner,
Not driving too fast
And as they did,
A beautiful group of starling birds
Flew out from nearby trees
They must've been startled
By the nest of bees
Over there,
She thought. They watched as they flew by
Slowing the car
But one bird must've not been able to fly
Quite so high.
They heard a thump
And her father gave a sigh.
"Please pull over, daddy!" she cried. He pulled the car over
With a feeling of worry
Over what they would find. She opened the door,
Her father followed
And they ran out to the nearby trees.
She looked to the ground
There was no sign of the bird.

She thought back to the sound.
"Maybe it was on the road?"
She asked her father.
But all they saw was an old, squashed toad.
They looked and looked
And couldn't seem to find the bird,
"How absurd,"
Said the father,
"It must be here."
"Maybe it flew away,"
Said the little girl
With her head full of curls.
He looked at his daughter, "Maybe so," he said
But he did have his doubts,
After all of his bouts
With happenings like this
They usually didn't end
With a happy outcome.
That day though the woods
Held something almost magical
Shades of greens
That seemed all so radical
June blurted out "mysteryical."
"Honey, that's not an actual word."
"But it is, dad, right? Mysteryical."
He looked out at the green painted forest,
"Sure, I guess it is."
As they turned and were about
To make their way back
June spotted a beautiful silver
Colored stone

The light seemed to tone the other darker colors,
So that its beauty made itself known. She picked it up
And noticed that it didn't seem
To fit here in these woods.
She asked her father if she could
Keep the stone
And he answered, yes if she would
Take care of it.
She agreed,
She could keep the stone
And her home became its home. After school that day
She rushed to see it
And spoke all she could say
To her new stone.
She looked at the beauty of it
And noticed the streaks of silver, how special, she thought,
There was a streak of purple
That seemed almost caught
Inside.
She talked with the stone
Every night,
And she would tell it how beautiful it was,
And all about her day
She also did happen to say
And share her dreams
Of travelling plans
To many different lands,
Stories that she had heard,
Adventures she had listened to,
From her parents in multitude.
She would look at maps and a globe

And go over the nodes
Of latitude and longitude
And list all the places
That she would one day visit.
A stone, she realized,
That, even though just a stone,
Seemed to be a great listener,
Her love for it had surely grown.

The next morning she woke
To find the stone was missing! How could this be?
She thought, it was just here,
Waiting for me.
She looked under the dresser,
It wasn't there.
Sometimes after she would talk with it,
She would place it under her teddy bear,
It wasn't there.
June sat on her bed,
She put her hands to her head
And cried.
What would she do now?
Who would she tell her stories to?
And share her dreams with?

Suddenly to her surprise,
She felt a light touch on her shoulder
Her spirits seemed to rise.
She heard a soft humming in her ear
She turned and looked,
And couldn't believe what she saw,

It was a beautiful bird
Sitting on her shoulder. She looked at it peculiarly,
Why, this bird wasn't like any other!
It had silver steaks in its wings
And a beautiful purple streak on its forehead.
Could it be?
That the stone she loved so much
Carried within it a magic she could finally see.
No, it couldn't,
How could it?
But she somehow knew
That the streaks that she found in the stone
Were the wings and feathers of this bird,
And the purple line on the stone,
Had somehow become the line on the bird's forehead.
That perhaps her stone had somehow
Turned into the bird that she thought was lost,
All she had to do was care for and allow
The bird time to heal,
Something she had done with her words
And with her comfort.
She began to talk with the bird
Once again,
Just like she had with her stone,
And the bird fluttered its feathers
And seemed to listen just like
When she and her stone were together, and even seemed to
talk back.

At breakfast that morning, she asked her father,
"How odd is that? That the bird

Did talk back?" And he answered,
"About as odd as the way
Those magical woods were that day."
Every night from that morning on,
June would leave her window open,
And she would begin her morning hearing a song
And the bird with its purple streaked forehead
Would come flying in,
And sit next to her and listen to her day,
June claimed that she also listened,
Because with all her travels, the bird had a lot to say.

But what of stones and birds that talk? They are stories told
From that magical forest
Perhaps from a time of old. The bird was real just like you,
And you can see it too,
All that's left is to close your eyes,
Go to sleep and dream
And a stone may one day seem
A little more colorful than the rest,
And you may take care of it
And talk with it, tell it your day,
Help it to feel safe in a way.
But just wait, in time
You may wake to find
Your stone missing,
And a fluttering singing songbird,
At your windowsill,
With a story to tell.

Missing Something

A pelican sat on top of an electric pole
Looking out into the world.
Down below, he saw a squirrel
Running back and forth,
From here to there,
And there to here,
He flew down
And asked him
"What is it that you're looking for?"

"It appears I'm missing something
Don't know what it is
Or where to find it
Or where to look
Would you know by chance?
Where to find what I'm seeking? I'm looking for some kind
Of something
I know it's out there
It will make me feel better
Satisfied and all together
Do you know where I can find it?
It must be here somewhere.
It's either round or small
Boxed or not
Maybe it's shaped like a ball

Or shaped like a square
It could even be over there
It could be here
Might you know where? I'll find it I will
I just have to keep looking
And looking and overbooking,
And unhooking latches of boxes
There must be something I'm overlooking
Maybe there's a clue
Somewhere around here
Will you help me find that too?
So now there's a clue I have to find
As well as the thing I had in mind. Let's look this way
Hmmm, now let's look over here
Don't mind the mess I'm making
It's part of the magic of being near We'll find it we will,
It's got to be around here somewhere
Keep looking and looking
Under the bookcase there
Around the corner down the stairs
When I find it I'll know
It will make me happier so
I'll keep looking, and will you too?
That way we'll have more of a chance
If two of us are looking.
We'll find it someday just have to keep looking
And looking and overbooking
Can you imagine it now?
How happy we'll be
Once we find the thing
That makes sense of everything

Maybe it's shaped like a triangle,
Or shaped like a star
Maybe I can't see it now
Maybe because it's too far
Maybe it's beyond all ideas
That I can even think up
We'll find it someday
Just keep looking,
And looking, and overlooking,
And overbooking."

"You'll never find it that way, silly
Overlooking means that you're looking over
The thing you're looking for,
The thing you're seeking
Must be something worth keeping,
It must be special
And mean a lot to you,
It must be essential
To being you.
What does it look like?"

"I told you, my friend
I don't know what it looks like
But I know how it feels
To find the thing
That make sense of everything, I know it might be square
Or it might be round
It will one day be found
It could be over there
Or in that jar,

Thank you for your care
In helping me find
The thing I'm looking for"

"Might it be something
That's already found
Found in that place inside you
Where joy abounds?
Where you haven't been to in a while
It's easy to miss
And is yet such a gift
With all this looking and looking
Let's begin to look inside
That's somewhere we haven't looked
And it does make sense
That place can sometimes be overlooked."

"Inside me?
How can I have the thing inside me?
The thing I'm looking for
Is the thing that makes sense of everything
It's the thing that will make me feel better
Satisfied and all together
It's probably grand and huge
And fills every room
And takes away all the gloom
And makes a big sound like boom!
How could that be inside me?"

"I ask you, my friend
To find a suspension

Of your disbelief
For a moment
Close your eyes
Let go of the ties
To what you think it is
And draw attention
To that space inside your chest
A place where you know best
Put your hand over that spot
And feel your heart beat
At the least it will give you a treat
Feel your breath rise and fall
It may make sense of it all."

He closes his eyes
For a moment or two,
Feels his heart beat
And beat
Faster then slower
Then seemed to spread all over
His own heart seemed to
Acknowledge and grow bolder
He laughed at the way
The beat shifted with his thoughts
Like a musical note
Played in a story
Only he could've wrote.

His eyes opened with joy
Wide and full of awe
When he looked inside and saw

That which he'd been searching for
And searching for,
"How could this be?
That all this time what I was looking for
Was just inside of me?
How funny a thing
This heart and light of mine
How seemingly small to the eye
How very tiny indeed
It seems it couldn't be larger than a seed
Yet it beats and beats
And plays this musical number
To keep me alive and moving
Even during my slumber,
How magical a sign,
This heart and light of mine."

The twist to this story
And the most amazing thing
Was that as he was looking and looking
And overlooking and overbooking,
The thing he was searching for
Was just in his grasp
It was there the whole time
All he had to do
Was redirect his mind
To his heart, to the light
To the inside
Where all life does coincide
At the time he just couldn't see it
Maybe it was just too far,

Beyond all ideas that he could even think up,
It wasn't shaped like a star,
Or shaped like a triangle,
It wasn't square
It wasn't over there,
It wasn't under the bookcase there,
It was much deeper
And much more special
And much more hidden
It took some time to get to
But he finally did find
The thing
That makes sense of everything,
It was the light within his own heart,
Something that he had
From the start,
He just forgot where it was.
And with that the pelican flew away
Promising to return one day
For he knew he couldn't stay
The next time maybe the squirrel
Would remind the pelican
Of the thing he was looking for,
And overbooking for,
We all need reminders sometimes.
Next time you look up
And see a squirrel or a pelican
He may be looking down
And if he approaches you
And you're looking around
For that thing that makes

Sense of everything,
He may be there to remind you
That you may be overlooking
The thing you're looking for
Stop and take a moment
Listen to the beats that you know,
And don't forget to greet him
With a smile and a hello.

The Time Traveler

"There's no doubt about it, I am what I am."

"And may I ask,
What are you?"

"I'm a director of finance
For a major corporation
I sort through deals
And help them into morbation."

"What's morbation?"

"It's a word,
That you would know
If you knew what I knew
And dealt with the blow
That comes when a company
No longer keeps track
Of their lack
Of important funds.
And may I ask,
What are you?"

"I am that too.
I am you and you are me.

We are the same, I'm afraid.
I just don't sit in an office
With my hanging accolades."
"Are you in finance too?"
"No, sir, I'm not,
I don't have a license
Or certification
Granted to me
By some graduation.
I don't have any letters, after my name
Granting some ability,
From where I came.
But I am you and you are me.
We're the same, I'm afraid."

"I am me and you are you,
We are different
Don't you see. In this world
To do what I do
And to be like me
You must go to class
Pass a bunch of tests
Be deemed worthy
Better than the rest. We are different
You are a lone pauper
With no attachment. I'm young and fresh
And crave amassment."

"I am you
And you are me
We're the same, I'm afraid."

48

"Well, that's not true, you see,
I have a fast car
And a big house
I have a front row seat
To the waves at the beach
In my five-storey mansion
That I paid for
With goals and expansion,
All the following through
I've climbed and climbed, made it to the top,
That's why I am me
And you are not."

"I've had all that
Made it up the mountain
Where I just sat.
I watched the fountain
Of youth disappear
in the far-off distance
It is very clear
Each one of us
Must face the great steer
Nod, accept and understand
That this is all
Just a temporary land. It's quite a sight
Up there so high
That view so blue. I do and see,
Just as you,
In my journeys I've learned,
All can create anew.

My seat to the waves
Is just like yours,
But it does sit closer,
And has no floors.
You and I,
We're the same, I'm afraid.
I've just been around longer"

"But sir, I am me,
And you are you
To do what I do
You need a blue
Permit saying you're true.
I have my own story
And you have yours.
I carry a briefcase that you adore.
I sit on the sunny side of this train stop
And you sit there,
Way over there in the dark.
My story's mine, for sure
For this there is no cure.
We're different you and I.
I am me
And you are not."

"Behind each sun
There are shadows
It's where I watch the most
Peculiar of fellows.
Fiddling with their phones
Staring into the distance

Waiting for some
Far-off call about business."

He sees nothing but
Here's the serene sound
Of the man playing his
Harmonica, homebound.

"What is that toy there? It looks so easy,
Teach me to play if you dare."

"I'll teach you a few chords
It will take some time
Before you play like me
And make the sounds rhyme.
I'll even give you my lucky one,
Here you go
It's black and has my initials
I'm guessing you like it so.

As I play,
And watch others
The sounds unite us all
In some common group of colors.
I am you and you are me
We're the same, I'm afraid
You just cannot see
Even though I travel this way
And you travel there
Our stories are just stories,
Created out of air

Underneath it all,
You will soon hear the call,
It's an expression
For following your heart
No need for impression,
Or to ask where to start.
Simply begin to be grateful
And you will see
Your life shows up much differently.

My hair may be gray
And my skin full of lines,
But smiles make my day,
And laughter leaves me cryin'.
And I know something
That maybe you don't, no matter where you go
Or who you know
Or what you own
Or what you grow,
There's really nothing to know,
And there's really nothing to find,
And nothing to sew.
The gold, unseen, is in the
Kindness of a stranger's hello.
We are the same, I'm afraid,
You and I.
I am you
And you are me,
Eventually."

The World We Forgot

"It's mine, all mine,"
She says, sitting under the last fruit tree.
"What's yours?"
"All of it, down to the rine
Anything and everything
It guarantees I'll be fine
This tree, it's mine."

"There is a confusion in this world
Of value and kindness,
And money and mineness,
It seems to have created a blindness."

"Now wait, Mr you
You can have one too
All you have to do is pay
And you can eat all day
Without money you cannot
Have anything in this world of not."
"What's a world of not?"
"It's a world of all the things
Where all is not
All is wanted and all is sought
But no relief for the seeker
Who always seeks

And doesn't find
Because what kind of seeker would find?
He wouldn't be a seeker of any kind."
"Maybe the seeker seeks and
Does one day find,
But in order to accept this
One must change the mind."

"Change the mind?"

"From one who seeks,
To one who finds."
"How do I change my mind?"
"It's simple really
Just think of a different way
Let the directions of your thoughts
Like a tree's branches sway."

"How will this change the world
From a world of not?
It most certainly cannot."

"Maybe it will not change the world
But for sure,
It will change the world of not
Into a world you perhaps have forgot
A world where all is asked for
And all is given
Where all is cared for
And all is forgiven
Where value is in kindness

Without a need for such blindness
Where we pay each other
With the things we create
And in the community
With caring we satiate
Made with our hands and with love,
With perhaps inspiration from above."

"Haha, what kind of world would that be
Without money, without time,
Without a leader to lead the line,
Without a clear definition
Of what is mine?
Things would go mad
People would too
Taking anything
And everything that they could
Oh, they surely would.
Without a clear definition,
Of what is mine and what is yours,
All would be quite chaos,
Yes it would.
Don't you think if there was a way to change this, I would?
This world of not into a world of could,
How funny, how mad,
How very sad,
That he thinks such a world of not
Could ever change into the world we forgot."
"What was the world like before we forgot?"
"It was just like you said,
A world where all is asked for

And all is given
Where all is cared for
And all is forgiven
Where value is in the kindness
No need for mineness,
No need for blindness
To the things we don't wish to see
Because everything we see
Is as it should be
Where the climb for money and power
Is not the rule
They are not even the attitude
Where nothing is needed
Because all is given
All are cared for
And all are believing
Where we share in spirit,
Soaring from you to me
And me to you,
Abundant energy
This is the world we forgot."

"How can we get back there?
How can we change a world of not
Into the world we forgot?"
She picked a piece of fruit from the tree.
She sighed,
"I don't know, my friend,
But just listening seems to make amends.
It surely has meant something to me,
Just talking with you

Has somehow seemed to set me free,
It's reminded me of the world I forgot,
I can finally see another way
Than a world of not. A world that clearly,
You have not forgot
I thank you for taking the time
And so, as I peel this rind
I'll give you half
Or more than that if you need
No worry for more,
We can just plant a seed,
There is no such thing as need.
No need for an attitude of greed
Because here all is asked for
And all is given
All are cared for
And all is forgiven,
Abundance rests
Within the seeds of our minds
All we must do,
Is look for the signs
Money is not needed
It plays no role really
In this world of clearly
All that we forgot."

She thanked him
And split the piece of fruit in half,
Gave one half to him
And smiled with a laugh,
As she thought how funny the world 57ould be,

When just one person could change her mind
So importantly.

The world she forgot
Was no longer a world of not
But became a joyous place
With no need to fight for space,
No need to win the race,
No need to plead your case,
Where all is asked for
And all is given
Where all are cared for
And all are forgiven.

Habit

A beaver sat on the side of a dam
And watched as the water
Started to build.
He munched and munched
And made his stronger,
Hoping he would have his home
A little longer.
He heard a voice
And popped his head up.
"I hope you don't mind me here
I was walking by, and I thought I'd say again,
Your dam here, it doesn't look
So sturdy,
Maybe this isn't the right place for it,
Also, it's a bit too dirty.
Could you try somewhere else?
I've seen you here before,
Weren't you just over there?
On the same waterway,
Didn't it flood the other day?"

"Yes, I was, I confess, I've been just a mess,
I lost my home last time,
And I just can't seem
To change this habit of mine

Of building in this one place
In this way,
I know, I know,
What you'll say,
Just go over there,
But it's difficult to change,
I seem to have this…
A habit, if you can call it,
A different kind of thing
If you saw it.
A habit of doing the same familiar way of it.
Of this, of that, of moving,
Of being, of feeling, of seeing,
A habit that I must've learned,
Long ago,
From whom I don't know,
And how did it grow
Into such a part of me?
So that it's become the screen through which I see?
It happened without me knowing,
It happened while I was growing,
And it's become this part
That I'm not sure is so smart
That I'm not sure is even a start
To being me.
It can keep me from asking for help,
It can keep me from eating greens like kelp,
It's just this funny habit,
I guess you can call it,
A thing I do,
And I don't know why,

Maybe it's something that made me cry,
Maybe it's something that I shoved deep down,
Maybe when I think of it,
It makes me frown,
So I try not to think of it,
And I try not to notice it.
So it just becomes this thing
That I carry around with me.
This thing that doesn't look like me,
This thing that doesn't fit in me,
This thing that is a mystery.
This thing that shows up
When I'm doing and doing,
And not noticing,
Moving like a robot,
Doing all the things I have to do,
And all the things I ought
To do,
And all the things that I was taught
To do.
How do I know the difference
Between a habit and what is truly me?"

"If it feels untrue,
Maybe it's time
To try something different and new.
Let the thing go,
Instead of letting it grow.
But first, to let it go,
You must look at it,
And become aware of it,

Watch it and stare at it,
Watch where it comes from,
Do you respond as a reaction?
For a satisfaction?
Watch what happens after
You do the habit,
Do you feel better?
Do you feel happy?
So that when you go to do the thing
You can try something different,
And you'll know why
When you try,
If it ends with a sigh,
Because doing something different
Is never easy at first,
Changing doesn't happen in an instant but may one day Feel
brilliant,
And just to remember
That as we grow, we change,
We rearrange,
We move,
We grow,
You will know if something
No longer feels right with you. This may be the habit
And a chance for you to let go of it.
Try something different,
Move on to a new way,
Say something you might not normally say,
And see how it fits,
And how it feels,
The next time you brush your teeth,

Use the other hand,
It might be neat,
Or the next time you read,
Read out loud with a funny accent
It changes the way we see
Just gives the mind a different
Kind of funny way to be.
The next time you pick up something
Pick it up with your left,
Or if you use your left,
Pick it up with your right,
And notice the sight
And you might
Realize what feels true
For you.
To notice a habit is something,
It's an inkling
A note to you
That something has stayed
Around longer than it should
Time to try something new,
Something new to do
Turn on a new light
That might
show you something
Magical and bright,
It may even lead to
A new way to see the world perhaps,
It can even make the brain a new synapse.
But first, you must let go of it, drop it down,
Let it fall to the ground

It doesn't have to make a sound
It doesn't have to be a big thing
It doesn't need to be a big production
Or a mass induction
Or a big reduction,
Just a quiet letting go,
With the courage to try something new."

"Well, now that you put it that way
I suppose I could try something new,
Maybe move to another place
A different space,
By the water of course, where the river is more calm
Where there are others
And I can feel like I belong.
Thank you, my friend,
You have helped me to see
A new way."

"Of course,
We all help each other,
Good luck, my brother, finding your home."

And the beaver and the squirrel
Said their goodbyes
And the beaver went on his way
And learned how to break
His habit that day.

A Christmas Tree is a Christmas Tree

"I don't know where she came from
But every year she's there,
Maybe not inside a home,
But always somewhere.
Outside, and when I roam
I see her there.

No matter where I go
No matter what I know,
A Christmas tree is
A Christmas tree, I know it to be so.

No matter if she's decorated
With lots of color,
Or if she's sitting outside
With her mother,
She may be in a forest
With the others,
No matter if she has lights
All around,
Or if people are making singing sounds,
No matter if there's Christmas cheer,
Or if I'm away from my dear,
No matter if the world knows it or not.
A Christmas tree is

A Christmas tree,
With one or not.

You see, the why of a Christmas tree
Cannot be bought,
And sometimes,
It cannot be taught.
The why of a Christmas tree
Actually matters not, because
A Christmas tree is
A Christmas tree,
Whether here or there,
Up or down,
Or all around.

Whether she sits in the ground,
Or inside a home,
No matter the where,
Or if Christmas spirit fills the air,
A Christmas tree is
A Christmas tree,
Even when life isn't fair.

No matter the why,
Or the questioning of how
She makes her way through
The coldest of winters
Through all the seasons too
With warmth, life and hope
For another day new.
It's almost peculiar how she does it,

The questioning can bring you in circles,
And sometimes the answer cannot be taught,
The why of a Christmas tree matters not.

No matter the who,
If people are making singing sounds,
Or if they decorate her with lights around,
Or if she's alone with roots in the ground,
Or if she's big and round,
I don't know how she does it.

The questioning can bring you in circles,
And sometimes the answer cannot be taught,
The who of a Christmas tree matters not.
A Christmas tree is
A Christmas tree,
No matter the thought."

"How is it then when there is laughter
And fun and happy times,
And then there is sadness too,
When people are hurt,
Or hungry,
Or passed on,
And we miss our loved ones and feel blue,
How does she carry on?
In the midst of cold and darkness,
How do her leaves stay green,
And full of life?
As if there is some secret unseen?"

"The questioning can bring you in circles,
And sometimes the answer cannot be taught,
The how of a Christmas tree matters not.

A Christmas tree is
A Christmas tree,
Even with questions sought."

"What if a Christmas tree has no lights?
What if she isn't decorated with colors,
Or given a star to place on top?
What if she doesn't look like the others?"

"I'll tell you, my friend,
Once again,
The what of a Christmas tree matters not.

A Christmas tree is
A Christmas tree,
No matter the why,
Or the how,
Or the where,
Or if there isn't a care,
Or the who,
Or the up
Or the down,
Or the smiles,
Or the frowns,
Or the tears,
Or the fears,

Or the worries,
No matter how cold,
No matter the flurries,
Or when you've gotten old,
No matter your beliefs,
Or the answers you seek,
Or when no one seems to be near,
Even without the lights,
And the colors,
Even without the star on top,
A Christmas tree with her
Secret to life unseen,
Her spirit surrounds her
In an aura of green,
Her promise for a new day
A symbol of life and hope
Learn from her we may,
There is life inside of her
Every day.

Whether here or there,
Up or down,
Light or dark,
Inside, or out,
A Christmas tree will always be
A Christmas tree
With one, or without."

The Fear Place

Inside the corner of a home
Sat two little mice
And each spoke twice
As much as the other
One of the mice was afraid to leave the house
To go outside to the garden.
She had seen others get hurt,
She didn't know what all
The fuss was about.
"I would rather stay here," she said with a pout,
"Besides, the way is blocked there, don't you see?"
The other mouse said
"Yes, but I've made a hole, I've been digging
And digging like a mole."
The other mouse knew
How beautiful outside was,
How she could meet other family
But this wasn't enough of a because.
And her friend knew how afraid she was.

"It's a safe place almost
It doesn't let our minds or spirits realize
That fear is a ghost, an apparition,
Acting like a separation,
And who isn't afraid of a ghost?

But the thing about ghosts is that they like to coast off of
other worries
So that the world begins to look blurry.
But the ghost of fear is fed by listening,
So if you must, give it a quick ear,
And then move along, let go of that song, and be on your
way,
But I'll just make sure, say, that fear can lie,
It can make you hide on the inside,
It can sound like a choir, in back of the thoughts,
Saying things that don't mean as they sound,
Whispering what won't happen, telling you about other fears
around.
Keeping you from doing the things you'd like to do, making
you question a feeling that you know,
Is true for you.
It can look like a wall, it can look like a block, it can look like
a lock,
Sometimes fear looks like a big bubble, waiting to get you
into trouble. sometimes fear looks like a door,
Sometimes like a kite that is reluctant to soar, or other times,
like a lion's giant roar.
Sometimes fear looks like the question, what if I have to talk
more?
Sometimes it looks like a clock, other times, it does not,
This is why fear is a ghost, sometimes there, sometimes not,
sometimes saying nothing,
And other times, a lot.
If you can see through the fear, through the shadowy holes,
To the other side, to the way that's clear, you can begin to
chip away at it,

Let the pieces of fear fall to the ground, watch as they
disappear,
Eventually you can see,
To the other side, to the way that's clear, you can see how
rickety the fear was, how with just a nudge,
The whole thing crumbles to the ground, with just the
sound,
Of the words, fear, you are not real.
You can see all the pieces of fear were just whispers in your
ear, from ghosts of the past,
Created
For you to see through and to find
A new way that's true."

And the little mouse began
To make her way
She tiptoed as only a mouse could
She whispered as only a mouse would
She looked around like she should
And she made her way to the garden.
There she found others,
And so much food too!
And shared it with her brothers.
The rickety fear that she had to walk through
Was just a piece of old wood
That must have fallen just then or again,
Or maybe it was way back when,
To make her think and feel
Like she couldn't face it when
She finally went outside,
But oh, what a ride
She would have missed.

The Weeping Willow

One day, a bird visited a weeping willow tree,
And as she was hopping from branch to branch, the bird could see
The tree begin to cry, and as she cried the bird
Asked "Why"?
At the risk of sounding absurd, the willow answered.

"I cry every day,
And every which way, up, down,
All around,
Tears they just come and visit me."

The bird was confused
And felt sad for the willow.
"Why? Why must you cry every day?"

"I don't know really,
If there is something wrong.
I think it's just a letting go
Of a particular song
To share the inside with the outside maybe
A way for me to be lately."

And the bird wanted to help.
"Oh, you don't want to cry in public though.

And make sure you use a tissue
You don't want others thinking you have an issue.
And make sure you smile after,
So others know you are okay
And make sure you have a reason
Or you can say it's just the season."

"What if I just want to cry? For no reason at all?
What if it's a way to say goodbye
To yesterday,
To the moment in time that's now,
To the questions of how
The beauty in the world happens
Every day,
What if I'm just sad,
For sadness sake,
Should I hold it in then?
Should I stop the tears again and again?

"It scares me so.
It makes me just want to get up and go.
To leave this place of uncertainty
To fly and never look back
Like there is some emergency."

"Well, you have to do what you have to do and feel what you
have to feel,
I know but for a moment direct your attention away from
the emotional throws.
There is something deeper you'll find,
Something deeper, maybe divine,

A place inside you where you can see
Sadness for who she really is,
A beautiful place inside
To get to know,
Not to fly from and hide,
She'll help you, she'll be there,
So that peace may abide.
She may even help you to see,
And you may finally understand,
How sadness can really a friend, come to be."

"Well, now that you put it that way, I don't really know,
I suppose it's okay to show
Sadness and tears,
Maybe it's just one of my fears,
To cry in front of others
And to show sadness."

And the willow continued, "I cry
And every which way, up, down,
All around,
Tears they just come and visit me.
I cry
Because I realize
That the real stuff of life
Was nothing that I thought it was
When I was a sprout
It's the passage of time,
The babies born,
Who will one day leave their nest,
Watching the sun rise every day

And set in the west,
Watching a bird work all day
And finally take time to rest.
Watching the hard work
That it takes
To make a nest. It's the people you love,
And the memories of old,
And the new beginnings
And the hardships
And the happy times,
And the sad times,
And the wishes and the dreams
It's all so mystical and wonderful it seems.
And I'm very old,
Maybe a hundred years fold. In a single tear,
There are so many words. So I cry to get them out
I suppose,
To share the words
Without speaking them, to share the compassion
For the fears while feeling them,
To share the inside with the outside."

And the bird understood, and finally felt sadness.
"That makes a lot of sense to me. Please excuse the tears
That now you see."

"Don't worry, my friend. It's natural,
A random sort of magical
Where the inside meets the outside. The tears and the fears
And the sadness will pass,
Just wait a moment

And let the tears amass,
They will come,
And now let them go. And remember,
I'm your friend, I'm here for you,
No judgement, no depends, it is okay to feel,
It's just a part of being real."

The bird saw what the willow saw,
And was grateful.
"I seem to have found a new way to be,
A new way to see,
And it'
s all thanks to you,
I see now that sadness is not Something to hide,
But a real part of being
'On this life's ride.
Just like joy and happiness,
Sadness needs her time too,
Its part of being whole.
It is okay to feel,
It's just a part of being real.
The laughter and joy will come again,
Just wait and trust
But sadness,
She is a must,
If I am to truly enjoy happiness again."

And the bird learned a lot that day
And if tears wanted to come, they may
Because she knew that all feelings belong
From then on she would visit the willow,

And sometimes her song
Was of happiness and sometimes of sadness
For she knew from that moment on,
That it was okay to feel,
It was just a part of being real.

Comfort

A salmon fish,
Wiggled his tail
And swam over to his friend
Without fail.
"The tides are rising soon,
The time is coming, under the moon, it's time to go, we must move
And swim upstream."

"There is a discomfort
There, so I'll just stay here. In my own comfortable place
Where I can see things clear."

"Why not come this way? You will learn much
And perhaps grow and such
I know it is quite a scary thing
To change, to grow, to rearrange,
But I suppose that's a part of the journey."

"Well, I'll just stay here,
Thank you very much,
I like it here,
In my own comfortable place
Where I can see things clear
You go and do what you like,

But, as for me, I'll be right here."

"Well, my friend,
I cannot promise that I'll be
Back around this way,
You see, I've found the courage
To face my fears,
Come what may,
So whatever happens to come
Onto my path,
I meet with courage
And a little sass.
But that's the thing,
About moving along,
And finding how to sing your song,
You have to move,
I don't know what will happen next,
Or where I'll be, or what I'll do,
But I do know that I may not
Be back around here, to you. This journey may take me
To other ocean floors,
It may take me
To different sands,
Different waters,
Or rivers, or islands,
I may even grow taller,
But I don't know if
I'll be back around here. So I'll ask you again,
My friend,
Come with me,
And we can see

And in this unknowing,
At least together, we'll be."

"I'm afraid, I suppose,
What if the waters rose? What if the wrong way
We've chose?
What if I make a mistake,
And learn that the place
We end up in, was all
Just because of our fast pace? This isn't a race,
Let's just stay here,
Where I'm comfortable,
Where I can see things clear
Why change things?"

"You cannot see this
From where you are,
But the waters are rising here,
There will be a flood within a day or two,
And you will be pushed out of these rocks.
There may be a storm,
This place was great for a while,
But with new thoughts born,
We must change, rearrange,
We have to move along. Why not come this way?
You will learn much
And perhaps grow and such
I know it is quite a scary thing
To change, to grow, to rearrange,
But I suppose that's a part of the journey."

"It doesn't have to be a part of my journey
Or yours as a matter of fact,
Long ago we made a pact,
To stay together.
We can stay here,
Where we are comfortable."

"For me, my friend,
The clearness is not so clear any longer, the place is not so
comfortable,
And I feel the pull is stronger, so I need to move along
yonder,
And find out how to sing my song.
I don't know what will happen next
Or where I'll be, or what I'll do,
But I do know that I may not
Be back around here, to you.
I want to see where this journey will take me."

"Why are you in such a hurry?
Like you are moving because of worry? Let's just stay here,
Where I'm comfortable,
Where I can see things clear."

"Then I'll be on my way, and I have to say goodbye, but I say
it with a sigh,
I'll miss you,
But I'll be moving along,
To find how to sing my song,
I don't know what will happen next,
Or where I'll be, or what I'll do,

But I do know that I may not
Be back around here, to you.
This journey may take me
To places that I can't see now,
To places that I can't see how,
To moments where all I can say is wow,
But this is the way, the Tao."

His eyes were saddened but he knew
That sometimes you have to walk your path alone,
And as he began to swim away,
He felt the pull further,
To go upstream,
So much so that everything
Felt right, it seemed.

Just like the salmon who have
To swim upstream,
Sometimes we have to
Go our own way, it seems.

Your Voice Matters

Two birds sat together
On a branch contemplating
Something about the weather.

The birds began to sing
And the one grew quiet
And the other could see
There was something she wanted to say.

"What is it? What do you want to say?"
'

"I'd rather not, please I pray.
It's just easier this way
Not to say
What I want to say."

"Easier?
What do you mean?"

"It's easier
Because things right now, they are okay,
They are calm, and good,
The way it should sound.
With my voice, I fear that I'll
Give a choice

To believe another way
Help another to see
Outside of the box I'll say
Maybe it will incite
A new direction
You might not like it,
And if that happens,
What will you say?"
Maybe you'll become angry
And not want to be my friend
It just might happen, it may
You could disagree
Could take it the wrong way
You could not really hear
What I meant to say
What then?
Then I will get nervous,
It just might happen, it may,
There may be a confusion
Things discombobulated
A miscommunication
In my computation."

"My friend
But you do matter too.
What is the worst that can happen? I get upset at what you
say,
That's my business, not yours,
If your feelings are kept at bay,
It almost leaves you without a way,
But when you share the song

That you feel in your heart
You are saying
'I am good enough
To say what I want to say, come what may,
To the world, to a friend
To that person there
To everyone wherever where.'
Even if there is a confusion
And miscommunication
In your computation
Even if you get nervous
And the song comes out a different way
Be that as it may
Those sounds come from inside you,
Trust and sing the words that are true
Would you rather keep it inside?
And let another miss the chance
To experience such a ride?
To give the chance to see the way you see,
Maybe what you sing will bring
About a new connection,
Some new kind of introspection
Maybe even inspire a dissertation!
To question,
To change,
To rearrange
This is this excitement
And delightment
Of sharing thoughts and songs
It truly cannot be bought
An exchange of thoughts

May bring about change
And things to be
Discombobulated
And resituated
But would you rather stay silent? And let that voice
Maybe grow violent? Just like muscles
When we exercise our voice
It grows
And your inside, it knows
So take a chance and share
Take a moment even
If like doesn't feel fair
And say what you want to say
Share it, come what may
If you say too much,
Maybe you say too little,
Maybe you say the wrong thing
And frown a little.
But those words come from inside you
Trust the words will appear
And what is true for you will become clear
Say the words, the ones you need to say
Because your voice, it does matter
Every moment, even today. Our insides have a way of
Making their way out
Coming from the inside out
Your voice is yours
It's the only one like it
In the whole world
It's like an arm or a leg or a wing
It has to be exercised and moved

And needs its rest too
And to be soothed
But it's yours,
The only one in the world like it.
The chance to choose
How to share it
Is yours.

And if you choose to keep it silent
Keep it hidden
You may find one day
That you may
Notice it's gone quiet
Maybe it's temporary
Or maybe it's longer than that
But it is a fact
That what you give
Your attention to grows,
So give some attention
To those words that you know
Maybe just to say hello,
Maybe it's to say no,
Let it rumble up from
The depths below
Until it travels all the way up
Making a sound
Unique to all others around
So share it,
Allow yourself to care for it
Maybe it changes things,
It rearranges things,

Maybe gives others a different idea
A new perspective of things.

But it's yours to share,
It's your choice to bear,
There is no cost for it,
No extra layers to wear Courage is not found in
Keeping your voice quiet
Or keeping it silent
But in saying the things that
May be difficult to say
That might cause a disarray
That might cause anger or upset
Even some mistakes along the way. And that's okay,
Because your voice is yours
It's the only one like it,
Coming from the inside out,
To express and be expressed
To show and be shown,
To share and be shared.
The words will appear
And what is true for you
Will become clear
Say the words, the ones you need to say
Because your voice, it does matter,
Every moment, even today."

I thought for a moment
Listening to these two birds talk
And I began to sing
Like I never have before

Like I wasn't afraid of what was in store
Like the little voice inside me
Suddenly let out this giant lion's roar
The sounds coming inside me
Just began to soar
Their song meant something special to me that day
It gave me a reason to share the words that I needed to say.
To express and be expressed,
To show and be shown,
To share and be shared,
Saying the words, the ones I need to say,
Because my voice, it does matter
And so does yours,
Every moment, even today.

The Turtle and the Fox

A turtle meets a fox
On his morning walk.
The fox seems to be lost.

"Hello, Mr. Turtle,
Well, I seem to be lost."

"But you are a fox,
You can get out of anything, you can find anyone,
And I've even heard you sing,
You run from here to there,
How can you be lost?"

"I have lost my family, it seems,
In some calamity.
And I may have hit my head
So I ask you, my friend,
As I seem to be lost,
And at my end,
Which is the way for me to go?
I was wondering if you knew where I was
In this strange place
Please oh please tell me
Maybe with a little grace,
Tell me who I am,

So I don't have to keep
Trying to understand,
Some days I feel like I'm in quicksand.
I was wondering also,
Could you tell me which road to take? This one or that?
Could you tell me
Where to go,
And what I'll need to know?"

"That you seem to be in a race,
But that is me, I tend to move slow,
I cannot tell you which way to go,
I cannot tell you what to know,
I cannot tell you who you are,
Or what to eat,
Or who you will one day meet,
Or what for you is a treat,
Or if you will like beets,
Or one day when you're given the chance
If you will choose or not to cheat,
I cannot tell you how to dance,
I cannot say what is right for you
In any circumstance.
I cannot even say where you are.
You may want to know and to see
But little fox, then where would the magic be?
For this is the search,
This is the living,
This is the giving.
I will tell you to look out
Watch for those who give the answers

Too quickly
Who seem to know
Too swiftly
For everything can be understood
More simply.
Listen with one ear
But turn deaf the other
For everyone
Even as close to you as your brother,
Is also finding their own way.
You may pick up a flower,
And see it as a sign,
And another may see it
As a way to resign,
To choose a different way
If you follow too closely
You may notice
Your inner voice, it can turn ghostly,
For you have your own way to go.
The direction you might not yet know,
It may lead you to this way,
And that way,
Making different turns,
These are just ways to learn.
You may feel lost and scattered
Almost like nothing matters,
But there is a way for you,
It may make sense of it,
It may happen bit by bit."

"But I don't know where I am, or where I'm going,

Will I be running? Will I be jumping?
Will it leave me sad and moaning? Will it leave me happy and
glowing? Will it leave me with a knowing?
And I don't know who I am, Am I like you,
Moving slow and steady,
Wise and always ready? Am I like that tree?
With the ability to see
Far and wide
I think I must be afraid, you see,
Afraid of death,
And even life, maybe."

"But my friend you have agreed, to this life before you came,
And that agreement
Is the same
As the trees agree.
It is one of a promise
That life will come as well as death,
So with my honest breath
I can't answer your questions,
But I know this for sure,
You will be growing.
All these questions,
Won't lead to your knowing,
Just trust in the going.
And what really is knowing?
It's just a way you have learned,
But it may not work
For others in turn,
For they have their own way to go.
So the knowing that you know

May to you look like a sign,
And to another as a way to resign,
Trust that the way will show you
Maybe even give a clue or two
Just find the courage inside,
It is there just beside
The questions of how,
And why
And who
And where,
It is just found there."

"Now I can see that the answers are just here, inside of me.
And they will come
As they are meant to.
And whichever direction I choose will eventually
Show the way for me to go.
I simply needed to remember
My own courage, just so.
As I sit here with you, and I ponder,
And in my thoughts, wander,
I realize now that I don't have to
Have it all figured out,
This agreement I've made,
Before I came,
May include the questions
Who should I be,
And what should I do,
The answers
Will eventually
Come as I go,

I don't need to always know
All I need is to remember
My own courage,
It's inside, just so."

I Want to Save the World

A little ant one day,
Found his way
Outside of his typical route,
He wondered, I'll say,
In his typical suit,
How he could save the world,
This thing was wrong and that thing too,
That thing over there was too big,
And that there, needed a rig,
And maybe we could feed all the starving animals,
And we'll have plenty of the aphids honeydew,
We'll even save the termites too!
He thought, we'll set up a huge machine,
In the sky, maybe that could drop food to all
Even to the smallest of small.
He thought and he thought,
How can I make this happen?
How can I save the world?
Is a good question and caption.

An older ladybug, he must've been,
Came and wandered over as he smelled for something sweet
and lifted his chin. "So you want to save the world?"
he asked with a grin.

"Yes, Mr Ladybug,
I want to save the world,
And I want it to be big and grand,
Maybe you can help me save the world,
We can do it; we'll surely need a big clan."

"I've tried in the past, like you, my friend,
With the same aspirations but it was all to no end, and what
I learned was this, to save the world,
It starts with me."

"But that's what I'm saying, don't you see?
It does start with me,
We can do big things,
Fantastic things,
Dig through the biggest tunnels,
Create bombastic rings.
But saving the world,
It's in the big things."

The ladybug nodded and said, "So, you want to save the
world,
But can you shake your enemy's hand?
Can you pick up that can
And carry it with all your hands and use it to recycle?
Can you be the first to forgive? Even after an insult?
And use that as a catapult
To send a prayer?"

"I want to save the world; I want to feed the hungry."

"Can you feed the ant down the street, who lost his family?"

"I want to save the world; I want to heal the sick."

"You want a lot of things, my ant friend,
Can you put a dressing on a wound for the ant at the shelter,
And come back to see him soon?"

"I want to do big things, I want to go here,
And there and help him and her,
Mr Ladybug, I have this feeling, I just want to save the
world."

"Yes, you want to save the world.
Can you help that old ant cross the road?
Can you make a meal grown from the food you've sowed?
Can you find love in the hardest of moments,
Can your heart stay open in the toughest of times,
Will you watch out for the other ants
As they scurry across the road?
Will you let go of the money owed?"

"We don't use money, you know that."
"Yes but you use something equal to it, no doubt. Can you
bring food to your neighbor,
While she is not feeling well, Can the words you speak
Be followed by your example
And the true life you seek.
Can the words you inspire
Be the same as what you are?
Can saving the world start with you?"

The ant thought for a moment or two, "If what you are saying is true,
I am just a little ant,
How can just me do anything to save the world?"

"When we take care of the things in our grasp, the things and the ants closest to us,
When we take care of our tunnels, and the soil around us,
So that eventually,
The soil will clean and replenish itself, a gift nature has provided,
Without much of our help,
The earth will one day sink so far into the ground, and show up on the other side of the globe,
And if you're not sold,
When we take care of our air,
We can choose not to spray chemicals, and if you dare,
Have plants that clean the air Because they do,
Recycle it too."

"But these are just small things, they are little things to do.
I want to do the big things,
And it will save the world, I'll prove it to you."

"Oh, my young friend, when will you learn,
That the way has always been in the everyday,
And those things you call small things, as you will see, will change and affect the big things, eventually."

And that moment, the ant, discouraged, went back to

digging his tunnel,
And as he did, he began to see how
His tunneling helped the soil around him,
And he began to see the roots of
Plants and flowers, abound around him. And how as he
gathered his food
From what some called garbage,
He was actually keeping the earth clean! And with this, his
smile started to beam,
As he realized he was already saving the world,
By doing his work,
In his own way, every day.

Your Different

A little black-and-white bird named Jack, one day at school,
Noticed he was different in a way,
He thought wasn't so cool,
He didn't laugh like the others,
Or walk, or fly quite the same,
He even thought his voice sounded a bit, lame.
He flew home that day,
Moping sluggishly away.

When he got home to his nest,
He threw himself into his bed,
And his mom arrived and
Said to him "Please listen instead.
That's just your different, you see
It's what makes you, you,
And mine makes me, me,
And sometimes
It makes us want to fly away."

"What's a different?"

"It's the thing that makes you unique,
The thing about you that isn't like others,
Your different is what makes you, you."

"My different though,
I don't want it any more, I want to be normal,
Like all the other birds, so
Can I just give away my different?
Why do I have to have one?"

His mother brushed his feathers aside and said, "You don't know it today,
But one day you will. I'll just say
Your different is what keeps you true
It's what makes you, you."

And after that day,
The little bird tried many ways to get rid of his different.

He tried to leave it behind one day
After he buried it in the dirt,
As he and his mom played in the park.

He tried to cast it away in his dreams,
Hoping it wouldn't be able to see in the dark,

He tried to let it go with a balloon
That he was holding at a birthday party,
But his different came back too soon.

He tried yelling at his different,
One day outside,
But his different was still there,
  He could feel it inside.

He tried on the church tower,
To pray his different away.

One day,
He even told his different to stay,
As he flew the opposite way,
But his different kept finding him.

He tried hiding from his different,
He hid around the corner,
He hid behind an old, large plant,
He hid under patios and chairs,
He even tried pretending to be an ant!

He finally gave up,
After his different found him again,
He let out a big sigh, and asked
"Why are you always around me, different? Can't you see
I just want to be like everyone else."
In his nest's corner,
They looked at each other, and he did feel badly.

"I'm here because I am you,
I am the you that makes you, you."

"Well, please just for tomorrow,
Stay home while I go to school.
I want to have one day,
Just one,
Of being cool.
One day to be like everyone else,

To fit in, and not feel like such a fool."

His different nodded
And the next day the bird
Flew off to school, half-hearted, without his different.

The day began like any other,
Young birds saying goodbye to their mothers.
But one thing Jack noticed in the classroom
Although he looked the same on the outside
Was that he felt just like everyone else finally!
At first he couldn't help but feel his beak smiling!
And as he noticed and talked to his friends,
He started to see their funny unique ways,
How Sally swaddled her notebook there,
How TJ actually looked like a big bear,
How Amy couldn't answer a question
But would always ask where?
How Lola would look off outside and stare,
How Julie seemed not to care,
How Michael had twists in his feathers,
How Suzy had a tick with her beak to the side,
And as I watched was just so rare,
How James who sat just beside
Always wanted everything to be fair,
On his desk in front of him,
Even colors of pens
He would equally arrange,
How even the teacher was afraid,
And kept a book on her desk called "teach if you dare".
He thought how strange

That he never noticed before.
And he realized that everyone had their differents with them,
Except him, because that day,
He had wished his different away,
He had asked his different to stay home. And with that thought,
He missed his different
With all of his heart.

After school that day he flew home,
And as he did he raced and called
Out to his different,
Asking for it to return.

He found his different in his nest just where he left him.
Out of breath he said "I'm so sorry, different,
I didn't realize what differents do for us,
They help us to be who we are!
None of us are exactly alike,
Because our differents
Make us unique in God's sight!
So please, oh please, stay with me today,
Keep me different and me,
Tomorrow and always."

From that day forward Jack and his different
Could always be found together
Unique in their own way, and I'll just say,
That when you find your different,
Make sure to keep them around,
In your busy life,

Your different is what keeps you sound.

The next day he brought his different with him. And he saw
his friend laugh and giggle,
Maybe out of context a little,
She looked up as the class all stared,
And Jack said to her,
That's your different,
Don't be afraid,
Your different is what keeps you true!
Your different is what makes you, you!
And they smiled with their beaks together
At their differents' funny ways,
And they promised to keep
Their differents with them, today and always.

Words

A mama monkey sat with her baby monkey,
As her baby began to speak, he had something to say.
"I don't like to use my words."

"Why not, sweetie?"

"They don't make sense all the time,
I would rather just stay quiet and use my hands and
Nod different ways. Words,
They are so complicated it seems
Sometimes there's a q
Where a c would be
Sometimes a k in front of an n
Like in the word knee
Sometimes things don't spell
Like they sound
Or they arrange themselves
Into a noun
Some words they can even cause me to frown,
Words they are ever changing
And rearranging."

"Like new words
That are sounded out
Suddenly they make sense

And are found to mean something
Like the word notebook."

"Is it a word
Or a thing that you write in? Or is it both?"

"Everything is a word and it
Is something else too
A way to see the world
And at the same time do
Things with the words, like verbs. Like the word ride,
Ride is a word
And it is also a word verb
To ride a bicycle
Or a tricycle,
Or even a unicycle,
And then these words
Are things,
Things to ride,
Things to interact with,
Called nouns."

"Why would they call things nouns?"

"It rhymes with frown,
And doesn't always mean as it sounds."

"Do they all sit on the ground?"

"Well, not all nouns sit in the ground,
Look at a clown,

A clown is a noun,
And can jump up and down."

"What about a sound? Is a sound a noun?"

"A sound is a thing... It is a something,
But not everything that is something is a noun."

"Then what is everything?"

"Everything is a pronoun,
It can stand in for a noun,
And makes almost the same sound."

"What about ice scream?"

"Well, screaming is a form of yelling,
A verb,
A way of telling.
Oh, oh, you meant ice cream.
That for sure is something different.
Ice cream is something you eat,
And a noun
And tastes very sweet."

"Who would ever name it ice cream?"

"I guess it doesn't sound absurd
It is iced cream after all
And with all the sugar
Can make you climb up the wall."

"What about a name? Is a name a noun?
Or a thing?
What if a name sings? Is it a verb then
Or an action again?"

"You do have many questions
My sweet! And that is such a good thing
A name can't sing,
But a person can,
And a person is called name."

"So is a noun the same?"

"I suppose a name can be a noun.
Now you're just clowning around
Of course a name is a noun,
And a noun is a name. But what is the same
As a name that's a noun?"

"The same?"

"Yes, what is the same as
A name that's a noun?"

"I suppose the rain is the same.
The rain is a name and is also a noun.
But it is also a verb, like in raining."

"So a name can be a verb and a noun?"

"Yes, I suppose by the way it sounds.
Just add the ing on the end,
And it makes a sort of compound,
That makes the name that's a noun
Also into a verb."

"Oh that surely is absurd!
Who made up these names anyway?
Verbs, and nouns and names of things?
And what are all these rules today?
Words are words are words are words."

"Well, words are not just letters on paper,
They mean things like this and that
And their and here,
Words can show love even
And show laughter too!
Words can show feelings
They can tell what you're believing
And can even tell when you're blue
Words can bring you connection
And friendships even!
Words they are a magical thing,
And magic they can bring,
With a word you can show what you need,
You can show what you're feeling,
You can even talk to a seed!"

"I love putting strange words together
Like a conjunction,
It has a function

If combining two words into one,
Or two ideas for fun!
Like the word and,
Or the word, wait, actually
We just did it there!
Or is the linking of two ideas
So it uses the function
Of a conjunction!
Words can come together
And even words can bring people together
Words like kindness,
And grace,
And forgiveness,
These words change things,
You can see it on your face,
Words that bring people together,
They are easy to say,
I'll start with you, if I may,
You are kind,
An adjective,
And also a noun,
If you make a kindness, Grace,
It's a word that you can't say
Without your entire self
Lighting up from the inside, Forgiveness,
It's a verb to forgive,
And let's face it, it's some thing
We all need to even live. All these words,
Are just letters until you speak them,
Or just words until you read them."

"And when you speak them
You can feel how it changes you,
So is a word a feeling?
Or does a word make a feeling?"

"A word that is a feeling too,
Is in itself quite true,
Because it means something to you!"

"The most important words,
If you are to always remember,
Of all these words I send,
And all the words to choose from
And all the words we can blend
When all words seem to
Come to an end,
Is to find, within yourself,
A true friend."

The baby monkey looked up at his mama
And snuggled a little deeper into her warm fur
And was thankful for all these words
So that she could show him
What the birds knew,
And the squirrels knew,
We all use words in our own way
They may not sound the same to some,
But they are for everyone.

"Across the way,
Outside of where the monkeys could see

There was this glass separating me.
I saw these two monkeys sitting together
They looked so happy
Looking at each other.
A mama and her baby it must be
I wondered what they were saying
Did they understand words like me?
Could they laugh too?
I felt nervous standing there
Watching them for so long. But I am just a kid.
I thought to myself. What did I know?
And then as I walked away, I heard them say "Hello"
And I stopped and put my hand on the glass
And the baby monkey put his hand up
As if just another daily task.
And I knew that I would remember that day forever."

To some, the monkey and her baby
Sounded like they were making funny sounds
As they had this conversation,
Funny sounds and grunts that didn't amount
To anything like words,
But to the squirrels and the birds,
And to me that day, we understood,
That words, even though
They are so complicated it seems,
To someone on the outside looking in,
Words can tend to sound different than what they actually
mean, they might sound like a grunt
Or like a bark or even like a sound you have never heard
before,

But if you just take the time to listen a little closer
you can hear,
That underneath these layers of feathers and fur,
Scales and fins, as it were, that we are all just the same.

Two Frogs Sat

Two frogs sat
On the side of a pond,
One noticed the other seemed worried more than usual,
And asked, "What's wrong?"

His friend responded, "I have this part of me
It's a part you may not
Even be able to see
When I feel it a lot,
I can even forget how to just be,
Some people call it anxiety.
Some days I want to go places
And instead of going,
I get nervous about spaces,
So at home I stay,
And then I regret not going,
And feel like I missed out, I get angry at myself,
And have this feeling of being without."

"I understand what that is, my friend,
I've seen it and felt it before,
That feeling, the one
Of not knowing what's in store,
And being afraid."

"Yes! So I sort of go somewhere else
In my mind, in my thoughts
Sometimes I go into the future
Sometimes to a thing that I just bought,
Sometimes I go into a memory,
And I feel so lost and caught,
It's almost like I freeze
And these feelings inside me
Don't have any place to go
Even when another frog says I have to just let go,
And move on, I know
But these feelings,
They seem to keep me stuck
In the same place of muck,
And I don't know how to get out of it.
Until something brings me back,
Some kind of good feeling,
Or familiar feeling,
Something that I know,
Maybe it's cuddling with my mom,
In her arms of feeling safe,
Maybe it's listening to a sound that's calm
Maybe it's letting myself be late,
Maybe it's humming or singing softly to a song,
And I come back for a time,
And I feel present here, where I am,
Until something bad happens again,
And I sort of go somewhere else
In my mind again and in thoughts I send.
I go somewhere else, I kind of pretend,
To be something different

To go somewhere new,
To leave this place,
And I don't realize when I do this too,
I'm leaving you,
And the moment,
And the experience of life
And all things true."

And the frog said again,
Looking down at his webbed feet,
"I have this part of me
It's a part you may not even be able to see
Some people call it anxiety."

"See, where did you just go?
You went somewhere else, I can see it,
In your eyes
In yourself,
And I do sympathize,
Because I do it too."

"It makes me feel uneasy,
And a little queasy,
Like being around new people
I act like I don't care,
But I am so nervous inside,
And I look off and stare.
How do you change it?
How do you not want to leave
The situation you're in?
When you get nervous?"

"I guess the idea is for me,
To allow myself to get nervous
And feel whatever I need to feel,
Explore the uneasiness,
Think of good things for the queasiness,
And most of all take deep breaths,
I even count to four when I breathe in
And count to four when I breathe out,
The uncomfortableness may still come,
No doubt,
The breath will slow it down.
But the idea is to make room for it,
Have understanding,
Even if to start, it's just a little bit,
You can't have the light without the dark,
So the opposite of what some people call anxiety,
Is there, inside you
It's as much on the other side as the uneasiness is,
But it's just the opposite.
Because you can't have one without the other,
Breathing allows you to find that opposite place
That safe space
Within yourself
That place a level of calm
The same as the anxiety part of you is,
And when you breathe you can see it,
It gives the space so you can feel it.
Sometimes the anxiety comes
From thinking you won't be accepted
With these feelings, whatever they are,

But if you just give people a chance,
Sometimes they surprise you
And who you are will enhance
With this wide world,
There are so many feelings to be had,
So maybe you are judging your own in a way,
So just for today
Feel the way you feel,
And let that be okay. Also, I do this thing,
I count from one to ten,
But I count things that I like,
When I count slowly,
Or even look at the ground if I'm on a hike,
Focusing on the little things brings me back
It's as if the simple things in my mind,
I somehow in my focus have a lack
But when I see those simple things,
I breathe more deeply
More slowly
It calms me,
It brings me to a place
So that the blurriness I no longer see
Makes me feel safe in a way,
In thoughts of simple moments, small rocks under my
webbed feet,
The slow ripple along the water,
Or the slow rolling of a wave, Watching a tiny worm move
Or reading words one at a time, can help too, it can soothe.
Reminds me to take moments
Slowly, to hear words rhyme,
To be grateful for those little moments

Brings me back to where I am."

And the little frog hopped a bit higher on hearing this.
"That makes so much sense to me,
I'm still nervously twitching inside.
So afraid I could cry.
Afraid of what exactly I don't know,
Maybe it's the anxiety,
This part of me
That I guess now you can surely see."

"Well, my friend, I can see your anxiety,
I can see the nervousness inside
And I'm still here,
I trust you and I am your friend,
No judgement, no depends.
I can see you,
The anxiety part is just a part,
Another part of what makes
Your beautiful heart.
That is what I can see."

"You mean, you don't see my nervousness,
After all that I told you
And all that I showed you?"

"I see you, my friend,
Underneath all that,
I see your spirit
Soft and quiet,
Honest and true underneath

All that, I see you."

And with that
The frog
With the part of him
That you may now be able to see
Began to hop and skip and jump
To lily pads
With this new ability
Oddly enough from that day on,
His color began to change from brown
To a lovely green
Some say this was how they knew that the frog
Finally let his whole self be seen.

The Ant and the Sprout

One bright sunny day
In his own lovely way
A seed sprouted himself up and out,
He felt for the sun but with a pout,
Felt the dark instead.

He looked around for some kind of clue
He searched for some of the sky's blue
He listened for a cow's moo
But all he found was stone,
He pushed and pushed
Trying to find his way to the sun

After a while he realized that he was as flexible as anyone
And not only could he push up
But he could grow with a twist and a turn,
He felt for sure,, even certain that he could grow tall
And that he would find the sun
He just had to keep reaching,
And maybe he needed a little help.

The sprout pushed and pushed
And finally he grew tired
He thumped to the ground
In the tunnel he had found,

And an ant came by
After hearing the thumping sound,
And the sprout, frustrated, yelled, I can't make it,
Don't you see!
This cement sidewalk,
It's too close, it's right in front of me!

The ant looked and responded,
Do what I do,
I just dig through,
And make a new trail
Just find another way.

But I am a sprout,
I am little and delicate
How can I get through such a heavy stone?

Maybe you don't have to get through it,
Try growing around it,
And then look for the light. What's the worst that happens?
You'll get there safely,
Besides, it's better than where you are lately,
So you hit a rock maybe,
And you get stuck in the ground, what I do is,
I just back out and turn around.

I suppose that suggestion is sound,
I've never tried it before
But if you say you have done it, I'll give it a try.

And little sprout without thinking

That he couldn't, without
Worrying that he wouldn't
Took another way,
He grew and grew
The most any sprout would,
The most any sprout could,
In his circumstances
The most any tiny sprout should
With the light he had been given
He thought to get to the sun
It would be quite good
So he continued to grow
And in his courage he stood
Phew! He felt quite tired
But he kept going
With all the strength required
Even without the knowing
He sometimes desired.
Until he felt the smallest glimpse
Of warmth from the sun,
He finally pushed through,
He broke through the little patch of soil
And let out a great big roar!
And what he saw
He had never seen before,
There was light all around,
And many different shapes and sizes
Of sprouts to be found,
He couldn't believe it,
He had made it through,
Where he could finally see the sky's blue

So much so that after he soaked up some sun
He grew taller and taller too!
Eventually he couldn't imagine
Not being on this side of the earth.
And he always remembered his ant friend
And how he had helped him to find his way.

Soon after
As the sprout who wasn't
So much of a sprout any more,
Heard an older ant walking by say
Who seemed familiar to him once more,
"Don't I know you?
For sure I have seen you some time before."

The ant was surprised,
"Yes! It has been a long time
And my, have you grown!
I met you many moons ago"
He said in an excited tone,
"I helped you find your way to the light."

"Yes, I remember! Oh my ant friend
You were so clever!
I have never been able to thank you
You changed my life, you know,
I was alone,
And you gave me a way to go."

"I'm glad I could be of help,
I just told you what I had done,

You found your own way."

"So what can I do for you
My old friend
You seem a little blue
Like something is wrong."

"I don't think you can help me,
But I'll tell you what's wrong,
You see, I'm stuck on this side of the sidewalk,
My family is over there,
But whenever I try to cross,
All these large dark things fall near me
I get afraid and I can't get through,
I have this food on my back that I'm carrying for them too.
Is there another way you can go?"

The tunnel I had dug is caved in
Those big dark things came down on it
And crushed it quite a bit,
That's the only other way.

I have an idea
Maybe it will help you today,
I have grown very tall,
How about your crawl
All the way up my leaves and
Your weight will help you gently fall
Over the sidewalk to the other side,
You'll get there and I'll bounce back
And then you can get to your family.

But why would you do that for me?
You could get stuck over there, see?
And it's been such a long while.

I consider you a friend forever
And I'd love to see you smile
Love and friendship binds never really sever,
You guided me and this is my
Way to thank you,
I help you and you help me,
This what we do, in this way, we are family,
Even though I haven't seen you
In quite some time,
A friend you will always be.

The ant all teary
Looked over at the sidewalk
And saw the other side clearly
He took a big breath and
Thinking of his ant family
Found the courage, to climb
Up the plant's vines
And as he made it to the top,
Just like the plant said,
It fell over the sidewalk like a bop,
And he remembered what the plant said,
"Now you have to be quick,
You have to jump as soon as you see the other side,
I'll wave to you when I bounce back
But no time for goodbyes."

And as the sidewalk arrived
He did just as he said and jumped off
And looked back at his friend, the plant
It looked almost like nothing had happened,
To a passerby,
The plant was just normally as it was,
Reaching up to the sky,
But as the ant was greeted by
His loved ones and his family
He looked back at the plant
And smiled a smile
That could reach beyond
The longest mile
It was a smile so big
That the plant across the long sidewalk, saw it
And waved his leaf in such a way
That to someone watching it may have looked like a breeze
of the wind made it sway,
But after that day,
The ant always made sure
To stay at his side of the sidewalk
A little longer
So that with just the lifting of his finger,
Their friendship grew stronger,
And he could say hello to his friend,
And they would remember how
With vines and leaves the plant did lend
His help to a friend in need.

The Parrots

A parrot sat on his perch, with something to say,
To his friend who seemed to be hurt, and he needed to say it,
today.

"I didn't mean to say, what I said,
And now I dread,
That you will never forgive me
What I said was said,
In some anger, in some sadness,
In some madness,
It was said without asking my heart first, it was said
With a sort of burst without checking twice,
I said what I said because I was upset
I said what I said instead
Of telling you how I felt,
I acted the feeling
And had my anger hit the ceiling and now I'm sorry
For what I said, at that moment
I saw the color red, I feel worse,
With what I said, I thought it would
Make me feel better, lighter,
Less pain,
More all together inside, but I feel the same, because I'm
feeling
The opposite

Now I know,
That spreading the sadness or the madness
Doesn't make me feel less sad, or make me any more glad,
I feel the hurt even more because I can see it in your eyes.

Next time I'll just tell you how I feel, instead of acting it out,
It shadows how I really feel from becoming clear
So you can't really see
And I don't have to be vulnerable with what I'm really
feeling, with what I'm showing,
Maybe this is, in some way, growing.
Maybe I'm ashamed of it, maybe I settled the score,
But I didn't check with my head, didn't check with my heart,
I don't know what I checked with, but I was angry from the
start.
And now I realize,
That I can't take back what I said,
I can't fake that I saw red
But I can say one thing that may help everything
What I want to say
Is that I'm truly sorry from my head
From my heart, from every part of me,
Even those that you can't see, please accept my apology.

The parrot looked at his friend,
"I understand
And I thank you
For your apology.
It means the most with those note I know you've thought of
me because of what you wrote,
How you shared what you were feeling in an honest sort of

clearing
Of all that you felt.
I'm sorry you were so sad and angry and mad,
I forgive you.
I think next time
If we talked through these thoughts together
It might be easier,
And help us grow closer instead of pushing me away with
what you might say.
And we can talk about how you're feeling, in an honest sort
of clearing
No need to act it out,
It shadows how we really feel.
And just remember,
That we all make mistakes
And we are all birds,
We've all had the wrong words sung,
And, I, the same as anyone,
Have felt anger and sadness."

"I agree, next time,
I'm feeling sad, or angry, or mad I'll check with my heart
and my head
And in my thoughts, every part.
And I'll talk with you before saying something
That I regret
Maybe it was just to see my upset
On the outside instead of feeling it, alone, on the inside."

"And no matter what the words, written or said before,
Know that you can make your words kind again."

And they sat together,
Looking out of their cage that day,
And maybe it's as the not wishing things
Were different in a way,
But they felt closer to each other than ever before,
And felt more freedom with what the future held in store,
And the parrot who had all the anger in heart,
Learned how to express how she felt from the start, instead
of pushing the other parrot away,
With what she might say,
The parrot learned how to use her words that day, and she
became very good from that day on,
At expressing just how she felt inside.

The Be-ing

One day two birds sat
On a branch
The one had been flying around all day
Turning here and there,
And even up and down I'll say,
There was nothing she didn't do,
And the other bird asked her
"You go from here to there
And even up and down,
But my friend, I see your frown
So why not stay awhile
How does that sound?"

"You have to do this
And that,
And that thing there
In order to be anywhere
Or anyone
But no, don't be too rare,
Not too original is what I mean,
You don't want to cause too much
Of a scene,
Oh my friend don't you see,
In our world,
You must do, to be."

"But what should I do? And what should I be?
What if I can't answer these questions
That you're asking me?
Do you have any other suggestions?"

"You could do this thing,
And that thing,
Make that thing,
And try these things,
Just as long as you're doing,
And make sure you have something to show afterwards
You don't want all of your doing to go to waste.
The only way to make it mean something
Is to share it and show it,
Then someone else will see,
And they will know too
That you must do, to be.
We all know it,
It's like this secret inside,
When we're little and sit beside
The grown ups and the big people
We see all that they're doing
We don't see them very often cry,
More times than not, you'll hear them sigh,
But never, oh never, just being and not doing
It's possibly the worst thing
Because as you will eventually see
That in our world,
You must do, to be. And you'll see it,
Maybe they're watching TV,

Maybe reading a book,
Maybe creating a reading nook,
Maybe thinking of what to cook,
For dinner,
Maybe they give a look
When you remind them to just be,
And stop doing
But they look at you with sadness
That says oh you just don't understand
One day, you will learn to do
And you will see,
Just like me.
And then you can truly be.
To truly be,
There is no other way
You must do this
And you must do that,
Do that thing over there,
Always remember, do and do
And with all the doing
You will never be through
Because there is always something to do!
So keep going,
And going,
And doing, and doing,
And one day,
You will find out why,
You did all the doing,
So much it stacks all the way up to the sky! Never enough
Just do and do
You can make so much stuff,

And then maybe buy more,
But the doing is never quite done.
We can even make the doing fun! But life, real life,
In our world,
You must do, to be."

"What if I just want to be here
With you today,
On this branch,
And we can just be if we may
And let all of the doing be done
Even if it is sometimes fun,
Just for right now,
Let the doing be done,
And just sit with me for a while,
Now, I can see your smile,
The one that comes from
The not doing place,
And we can share in this space
Of not doing."

"But don't I have to keep going,
And doing, and doing
Because there is always something to do,
It's like this secret inside,
Then someone else will see,
And they know too
That you must do, to be."

"I don't know much about doing,
But for now,

Feel the branch below your feet
Hop a little up and down
Smile and frown,
Maybe dance around the being,
I've learned and maybe you will too, can't be earned,
The doing is in the being,
And this allows happiness to return, or so I discern."

"Maybe one day I'll learn,
But for now I'll sit with you for a while, feel the branch
under my feet,
Hop a little up and down, smile and frown
Maybe dance around."
And as he did, he started to feel
The edges of the branches below his feet, and he yelled
"How neat!
I can feel the edges of the branches!"

He started dancing around,
His toes curled, a smile appeared on his beak, and he had
finally found,
Even if for just a moment, what it meant to just be.

Printed in the USA
CPSIA information can be obtained
at www.ICGtesting.com
LVHW090951151023
761044LV00009B/469